JOY IN THE BELLY OF A RIOT

Poems, Prayers, Memories, and Meditations

BARBARA FANT

AMISTAD
An Imprint of HarperCollinsPublishers

Without limiting the exclusive rights of any author, contributor or the publisher of this publication, any unauthorized use of this publication to train generative artificial intelligence (AI) technologies is expressly prohibited. HarperCollins also exercise their rights under Article 4(3) of the Digital Single Market Directive 2019/790 and expressly reserve this publication from the text and data mining exception.

JOY IN THE BELLY OF A RIOT. Copyright © 2025 by Barbara Fant.
All rights reserved. Printed in the United States of America.
No part of this book may be used or reproduced in any manner whatsoever without written permission except in the case of brief quotations embodied in critical articles and reviews. For information, address HarperCollins Publishers, 195 Broadway, New York, NY 10007. In Europe, HarperCollins Publishers, Macken House, 39/40 Mayor Street Upper, Dublin 1, D01 C9W8, Ireland.

HarperCollins books may be purchased for educational, business, or sales promotional use. For information, please email the Special Markets Department at SPsales@harpercollins.com.

harpercollins.com

FIRST EDITION

Designed by Jennifer Chung
Title and part opener pages background art © Aleksandr Matveev/stock.adobe.com

Library of Congress Cataloging-in-Publication Data has been applied for.

ISBN 978-0-06-344789-9

25 26 27 28 29 LBC 5 4 3 2 1

Moore Black Press is the press for the radical Black imagination.

We are forging the future of poetry at the highest level
and cultivating the unexpected and the beautiful new.

mooreblackpress.com

i keep trying to write about the trauma,
but the joy won't let me

"joy is not the absence of pain, but it's happiness in spite of it"

Lupita Nyong'o

TABLE OF CONTENTS

I: IN FLIGHT THEY MUST SEE THE SIRENS: BELLY

in flight, they must see the sirens	3
we could be a Sunday, a Hallelujah, and an Amen	5
I still go to sleep with a chair by my door	7
Magic Before/Before Magic	8
bless the children	12
remember that body that was found, across the street when we were on our way to school?	13
when they say murder	16
And the bullet still got caught in my grandmother's hair	18
there will always be the tears that fall	24

II. I KEEP TRYING TO WRITE ABOUT THE TRAUMA: TRAUMA

when we say "murder"	27
i keep trying to write about the trauma	29
one day he will be waiting for me	31
and tomorrow you will be the boy I used to know	33
We will always be the mild mannered children	35
I have heard you may not come	37
Just the Two of us Girls in Plaid Skirts	40
when they said sick	42
I keep trying to write about the trauma, but the joy won't let me	44
Running	45

III. WHEN IT ALL WENT TO FIRE: RIOT

Roses for Bea	51
Angels for Ray	52
Never Call the Police	54

Hands Up: Someone's Praise	56
How much he wanted so deeply for me to be an obedient wife	58
I think of the girl in the green dress	60
House of Dust	63
May Dies in April	67
i am not my grief	68
how do I tell you everything and keep myself from spilling?	70
When it all went to fire	72

IV. THERE MUST BE ANGELS WALKING WITH ME: JOY

I am not what my family has done	77
if not this river and ocean	78
what is a body except to be	80
When she says "my body"	82
I choose to heal because I can	86
Too much/No one can tell me Nothing: An Ode and Elegy for the Perm	88
you are a prayer	93
there must be angels walking with me	94

V. HERE IS WHERE I THROW UP MY HANDS AND TELL MYSELF TO DANCE: AND JOY STILL

give me a home	101
here is the surrender in forgiveness	104
a new appetite	106
may we never forget to hold fast to who we are	108
I choose to live	110
bless the child	111
there is a way to be whole again	113
be the joy	115
Acknowledgments	*117*

I: IN FLIGHT THEY MUST SEE THE SIRENS

belly

an internal cavity

interior

place where something is most deeply ingrained

IN FLIGHT, THEY MUST SEE THE SIRENS

                                                  sing a song only they recognize

                                                  in flight

                                     they must see the sirens

                          before we hear them

                   smell the blood

                      before it rests

              on our shoulders

                        our hands

                                our sons

                 when the grass grows back

            over where the bodies have been,

do the birds find rest there too?

do they sing amongst the trees,

make a game out of the helicopters?

witness the breath of the children?

say a prayer for the loved one whose life was taken too soon?

surely the birds must know,

surely the birds must have something to cleanse their eyes

be feathered with a grace that erases bloody memories

have the courage to still

wake up the next day

find the strength to fly

WE COULD BE A SUNDAY, A HALLELUJAH, AND AN AMEN

a million suns breaking under
the day like a kite dancing in the sky
the hem of a skirt slicing the wind
on a Sunday
we could be a Sunday
a hallelujah and an amen
your mouth, an open bible
every scripture, another breath
we could be the breath

your eyes, my every tomorrow
we could be exactly what you need
a wine glass spilled over
the light, as we're both fumbling
in the dark, trying to find the next steps
we could be each other's next steps
a phone ring just to say hello
guessing the samples in each new song
a dance in the middle of the street
on a Tuesday at midnight

there was a time, where my every heart
was midnight
a broken cathedral of stars weeping
out of my chest
like thunder in a cloud
not even God came back for
we remember Lot's wife
a longing for what was
a mourn for what I've never had
a yearn for the rib I could become
breath into nostril
breath into bone
flesh of someone's flesh
I could be that for you

trust is a song I often forget the words to
love is a dance I am still learning
my feet often sway in opposite directions
but somehow
with you, they always point
towards the sun

I STILL GO TO SLEEP WITH A CHAIR BY MY DOOR

we could blame it on the trauma, I guess
the many times breaking and
entering was something I could not
control, the body has several openings
the soul, one door
a chair sits at the mouth of the long hallway
perched at the edge
the apartments I stay in do not
open to the streets anymore
there are always elevators, floors up,
a journey you have to take
to get to me
I like to keep it this way
no easy access
no quick way to enter
no fast way to flee

MAGIC BEFORE/BEFORE MAGIC

We have been called magic before,
Our eyes, subtle stillness, dancing to the branches of our bodies,
Our bodies
tree limbs reaching towards Heavens,
above the sun,
above the rain,
dance rivering us out of our bones,

We have been called magic before,
Swinging from trees until we became them,
Bearing the fruit of someone else's child,
nursing someone else's child while ours lay hanging,
its body, a box of bones we're forced to carry six feet beneath our chests,
So we dig deep
inside our bodies and pull out every ounce of glittered prayer glistening
until it reaches our tongues, and we learn to speak life over ourselves,

We have been this magic before,
Bursting into everyone else's box of glitter and shine
and hiding the fact that we birthed it,
it came from our womb,
we lay bruised and bloodied while they dance into midnight

until they become the stars we own,
We do own the stars, ya know,

We have been that magic before,
How else could you find something to wish upon in this shade of midnight
if it didn't already come sulked in our skin's shade of brilliant,

We have been this magic before
Teaching the moon to dance and bend her dust into the shape of an eye,
peering out onto everyone's breath while they sleep
to make sure they keep breathing through every ounce of night that hits their lives,

Like,
My magic is so black,
she looked in the mirror and called herself solar system
My magic is so black,
the stardust grew herself a fro,
braided her body into cornrows
My magic is so black,
she bounced her reflection off the ocean and the waves started sea-walking
My magic is so black,
her midnight's blues mistook her throat for hip hop, and jazz, and poetry, and mystery, and religion, and art, and culture,
and culture,
and culture,
everything stolen from her body's magic in the first place,

Where culture was ripped from our veins,
we learned to river ourselves into a chandelier of cardinals taking flight,
cutting the sky into red until everyone learned
how to bleed the rhythm of this nation,
We are the rhythm of this nation,
In all its black and brownness,

Black history is American history,
America does not exist without this hue of sand
and wood and tornado, and casket
We have learned to carve the caskets from our own bodies
and sing a new song louder,
carved the caskets from our throats
and bloomed a new tongue,
There is always a new tongue to be bloomed,

And we have always been this magic,
We have been called this wishbone and golden before,
But when they forget our names,
and they will,
because they do, often,
Every ounce of glitter left in our bodies will rise into a new body,
And throat,
And tongue,
Until we braid ourselves into a new language again,

Rewrite history again,
In all that magic
And rise,
And rise, and
Rise

BLESS THE CHILDREN

bless the children who grow up too soon
bless the limbs that must grow into bones that break
forced to be fruitful
then multiply
fruitful
and then divide
when the berries turn to blood
the grass to daisies flailing in concrete
be the stone that holds the soles
of the bodies that never got a fair chance at life
someone bless the child's life
bless the children who are no longer at home
bless the children who no longer know where home is
bless the babies
every child be someone's baby
bless the children
that are here
to transform the world

REMEMBER THAT BODY THAT WAS FOUND, ACROSS THE STREET WHEN WE WERE ON OUR WAY TO SCHOOL?

we were just kids

bloody footprints on the floor
all the shootings at the corner store

didn't we just leave?

yellow-taped spring flowers
how it is winter in the streets

we were just kids

remember how we did drive-bys with water guns?
reenact New Jack City, Boyz n the Hood

remember how she taught me to hold
razor blades around tongue?

when you see a strap, don't run
never let them smell the fear on your breath

remember that body that was found, across the street
when we were on our way to school?

didn't we know that dude?
we were just kids,

remember Jay's house? how it got raided and she moved away?
how we used to play, Barbies upstairs in her house?

how they turned her father into a firework
but it was not July,
   remember   how he survived?

still can't believe Nia is gone,
snatched her life in her own home
we used to braid each other's hair,
and teach each other dances, back then,

we were just kids

two motherless daughters
trying to teach each other,
how to be strong
how to just be

we were just kids

remember how we had to bend down
sit low on the floor and be quiet,
once the bullets started a riot in the streets?

staying away from windows,
fidgeting doors

we knew how to be still as statue,

we were just kids,

learning our innocence
and trying to hold it in our chests

praying the pastors don't rest,

praying the protections don't fail

tonight

we want the chance to live

we wanted the chance to live

we were just kids

WHEN THEY SAY MURDER

they mean *Black Body*

blood rain in Spring

summer children with no voices, snipped

petals stuffed in the mouths of all

the bodies   we birthed,

they, curse

they, hex

they, hunt

they, try to define

when they say *murder*, they mean

"our children"

bodies   who do not look   like their children

when they say *murder*

they mean *blood on everyone's hands*   except theirs

they, *toss gun*

they, *what gun?*

they, *gun on person/body*   found

they, *big large gun*
they, *big black gun*
they, *big black gun on big large black body*

they, threat

when they say *murder*

they mean, *threat*
fear
life
deserved

to be taken

AND THE BULLET STILL GOT CAUGHT IN MY GRANDMOTHER'S HAIR

my rage is a loud scream
no throat is strong enough to hold
my stillness has been paralysis
everything in my body went numb
unable to move, march, mobilize, or mumble
all the trauma triggered, the personal trauma
and all the words became a swollen fist
in my chest,

and I mourn every Black death at once
Ahmaud, Breonna, George, Tyre, Henry
too many names to name,
every body is a hashtag
every hashtag is a body, a life,
a parent, and a friend,
all the people in my neighborhood that never made the news
the houses that were set on fire
the crack houses I lived next to
and Brian, and Eli, and Shanice
who were victims of a system
that swallowed them whole

How do you choose life when life
chokes the life out of you?

and we still can't breathe
how you murder our mothers and our sons
and we are supposed to stay silent

the streets are on fire
and I want to burn them too
want to burn down every institution
until they shout that people who look like me
have a right to live

every microaggression from white co-worker,
from touching my hair to ignorant comment,
to saying I slammed a door when I didn't,
to saying I was arguing
when I wasn't
to telling me I'm too incapable for the promotion
but giving it to the white girl with less tenure
and less education than me,
and then telling me to take on half of the workload
that she can no longer handle from said promotion,
to her shouting "Rednecks lives matter" and laughing,
and telling me the youth are out here killing each other,
to lies and more lies,
to white tears and more tears,

to always the protection of the white woman,
to always forgetting about the Black woman,
to leaving the organization because my Black life
could no longer take the weight,
to leaving jobs so that I could save my Black mind,
because the stress is too much,
because violence begets violence
and the ghettos we love
are the ghettos you created
and the bullets still fly
and the bullets still rang
and the bullet still got caught
in my grandmother's hair and skull,
and because my daddy is healing,
and because his mind,
and because my momma worked so hard,
and because horrible food and all stress
and because cancer
and because she was no more,
and because now I am still trying to pick up
the pieces with my three degrees
and all my teeth showing
and yet still, you remind me
that my life is nothing, meaningless,
because you kill our sons and our fathers
you kill our mothers and our daughters,
and the streets are on fire

and because you won't even think
about the infrastructure of your building
or whose bones you crushed to build it,
until the whole thing burns
until the truth is shattered glass
in your mouth
and the whole thing burns

into smoke
an exhale from my mouth
and yes, this too is a protest
I saw my father today
I fell asleep to the sound
of my niece's laughter
I took a nap in the middle of the day
and dreamed about MarShawn,
and all he did was hug me and
never said a word, and this too is a protest
and Amber's smile is the arch in my spine
I rested my mind
sat out in the sun
went for a run
drank water and ate a plum
cooked myself a meal
wrote a poem
caught a breeze on the porch with
my 85-year-old mentor

read a scripture
listened to a sermon
turned Beyoncé into a sermon
twerked until my thighs hurt
braided my hair and then
rebraided it again

and this too,
yes even, this too
is a protest for my Black life
we birth children
load pistols
raise nations with our tongues
make meals for our families
march the streets
tear gas and mace in our eyes
and still
we make it home by sunrise
keep watch over our babies
after the streetlights
have gone out
and there is nothing but rifles
glaring from rooftops
we harness the protest
in our throats like a prayer
feel the revolution

become a flame
in our mouths

and watch the whole thing
burn

THERE WILL ALWAYS BE THE TEARS THAT FALL

the cleansing that comes
before the healing
the torch that splits the wound before
it lights the path

                        yet this is the unveiling
                    this is the unruly road that
                      winds itself into narrow
                          a thorn in side
                puncture in the round of the crown
                        this is our undoing
the unravel until we are braided back together

this is love
that loves us back
the birthright of our every breath
the forgiveness that spreads itself
wide across our backs

            the spine, that had courage enough
                    to grow wings

II. I KEEP TRYING TO WRITE ABOUT THE TRAUMA

trauma

an injury

emotional distressing or disturbing experience

wound

WHEN WE SAY "MURDER"

we mean *stolen*

snatched

a *taken* that was not yours to take

life gone

life ripped

lights out

on a bright that you did not birth

not yours

when we say *murder*, we do not mean *kill*

we mean *planned*

we mean *years of racism lodged in the pistol of a neck,*

barrel of your blood

we mean,

you will answer to God,

for all the blood of His

that you spilled

I KEEP TRYING TO WRITE ABOUT THE TRAUMA

but the joy won't let me
bend into anything other than the light
i keep stretching myself into a thousand midnights
and i awake amidst a million stars
sometimes the journey towards healing
is louder than the healing itself
the walk towards becoming whole
is often the fight of your life
here is where I fight for my life
here is where I see myself as more
it is much easier to dwell on the past
to recall all the places where I lost pieces of myself
rewalk all the streets collecting lost limbs
yet here I am claiming wholeness from my tongue
even when my body may not feel it is true
here I am, claiming freedom, when all I have known
is bondage, here I am free
offering myself another chance at actually living
offering my heart another chance at beating
offering my soul another chance at finding rest
even while I am still in this body
my pen wants to keep rewriting all the things

I have survived, the many lives I have lived
but the joy is forcing me to reimagine a future
the joy is forcing me to claim a future
the joy is calling me into a future
the joy refuses to let me
bend into anything other
than the light

ONE DAY HE WILL BE WAITING FOR ME

standing there, in the back of a room
after I have just finished the poem, ready
to take me for food or coffee,

one day, he will be there,
checking to see if I made it on the plane okay
wondering if I made it into my hotel safely
or when I am arriving back home

one day, he will call,
just to say hello, to let me know how much
he has missed me during the day
a bouquet of yellow tulips, just to let me
know it is always Spring when we are together

every flower an open door
every new petal a chance we decided to bet
on each other, one day we will bet on each
other, call each other to pray in the morning
write our gratitude lists and sing them
into each other's arms, like a braid,

he won't care if my hair is braided, or straight,
or shaved all the way to my roots,
he will be rooted, one day, some day
we will have a place to water and spring forth
from, to bloom from each other's kind of easy

Sunday love, one day, it will be Anita Baker
playing in the morning on the record player,
me two-stepping out of the shower, hitting
a dance move as I turn the corner, and him
there, catching me by the arm to hit the same

rhythm, and for that moment, we are in sync
the summer breeze blowing through the open

singing *"giving you the best that I've got"*
for you, *"I bet everything"*
someday, someday
he will be there, betting, singing, waiting
for me too

AND TOMORROW YOU WILL BE THE BOY I USED TO KNOW

how we met was sweet
I admit I was in a vulnerable place
searching for a soft slate to be soothed
      and you provided all the soothing
the night we met, I was not supposed to be there
and you had missed your flight earlier that day,
so we could call this divine
we could call this chance
we could have called this miracle waiting to happen
you asked for my contact
and messaged me right away
lunch date the next day and an ocean of compliments
to drown in
      am I supposed to feel this way?
I needed an escape,
and you were willing to provide
for months, we never let a day pass without a text
or a call, we never let too many moments pass
without hearing each other's voice on the other end
how easily this space can become quicksand
when all the red flags
are lenses the shade of roses glazed upon your eyes

like scales,
> *who will knock me off this horse?*
> *have I fallen yet? or am I still falling?*

there are triggers you have still failed to learn
there are signs I shouldn't have missed
> *are we friends? or are there too many cities between us?*

all of the trauma is shaped like a new city
every tear is a state
fear is now a country between us
and no one can read this map
> *who will we be to each other tomorrow?*
> *how can we know when we do not yet know ourselves?*

when we are still learning the people we want to become
when we are still learning the people we are
today we will talk on the phone
I will send you the letter falling out of my mouth
like a song, our todays wrapped in a cloud
in this moment, we can float,
> *if only for today*

WE WILL ALWAYS BE THE MILD MANNERED CHILDREN

You, the mild mannered boy
Me, the mild mannered girl
Always sailing
Always the sea
Always the ocean
Always the boat
Grief is a funny thing
You will heal, this I know for sure
Our mothers, both turned into a language
we weren't supposed to ever have to learn
A language too large for our mouths
A disease, we should have never had to announce

We know the stage and the page
I wish you would have come to Thanksgiving that year
I wish I would have given us more time
I wish I would have been a whole person, when all you wanted

was to hold me
13 years later, I will return back to the east coast
past the time that we would have been
and now you speak of children

Of fatherhood
A marriage that holds you together
I'm sorry I couldn't hold you together

Me, shy girl
My heart, a sanctuary of Sundays
you, reasonable
life as it comes,
Murphy's law
Karma
my faith, a jawbone
a sack full of teeth
a Sunday outlined in chalk
a sorrow full of Mondays
a tuned out record full of Tuesdays
a Wednesday washed clean of us
poems turned into mouths
dance floors under a bright tomorrow's sky
will tomorrow still wait for us, you think?
is there another tomorrow, for us?

All these poems about you,
Will I ever wring them from my skin?

I HAVE HEARD YOU MAY NOT COME

that your limbs might not push up tulips
into the earth's mouth
I miss you like you never left,
windows down, cool breeze
slicing through our hair
careening through festivals, stages, all
the stages built for us to remind
the world why we spend so much
time molding our thoughts on paper
walks at midnight, sunset the color
of my granny's cheeks, my big cousin's
bright nails, as she would run outside to
meet her boyfriend, Dwight, and his friends,
when we were young, they used to fill up
water guns and do drive-bys ,
chase us around the neighborhood,
switch up cars just to catch us off guard
like the year, we ran around blasting
Donell Jones' track *this is for my playas
in the hood… it's just an ordinary day…*
that was the summer Trey was killed,
right on the corner, three houses down
one house down from us was a crack-polluted

garden, and to the other side, the guy
who sold to them, our sun-filled days
were spent over my auntie's place,
bike rides through the park and
random strolls to the corner store
Dairy Queen trips were always a must,
just so we could clown Dom for getting
cherry Mr. Misties instead of ice cream,
as my limbs grew longer, it was buying
the cutest crop top and wearing it to the mall,
so I could give my number to a cute guy,
and buy the next cutest crop top for the next weekend,
skating or movies, a date or night with my friends,
my momma was still alive back then,
and I always kept one night of the
weekend just for the two of us
Oh Summer, I heard you might not come,
I miss your nights, thick like *Blackberry molasses*,
one of the things that never change
I kept that song in constant rotation,
like a Ferris wheel,
my mother's favorite dream,
the year my little cousin was born
was the summer right before my mother
flew into eternity,
sometimes, I would catch that little baby
gazing above my head and giggling,

as if an angel was floating above
making her laugh,
babies are so close to Heaven
it's as if they can see the earth,
melt into the sun before she
buries herself into a moonlit,
plum sky
Summer, I hope you come
back to us,
we need your memories
to remind us
we have once lived
and are still alive

JUST THE TWO OF US GIRLS IN PLAID SKIRTS

For J.S.

I came across your picture today
us in high school, smiles as bright as tomorrow
we thought we had so many tomorrows
back then, we were just two girls
drifting through school catching laughter in our hair
remember how we used to braid each other's hair?
we would stay up all night watching music videos
and tending to each other's crowns
remember our dance moves?
we'd learn every new move from Ciara or Destiny's Child
and plan to replicate it onstage

when I got the news of what happened to you
I was in a city three hours away in a classroom
learning about genealogy,
the patterns traced through a family line
my goodness how our trauma follows us
they told me of the house, that it happened early
in the morning
that your boyfriend didn't make it either

how they left the baby untouched on the bed,
swimming in a pool of blood,
surrounded by parents she would never grow to know
her only memory, a lullaby of bullets springing
out around her, a fireworked nightmare
they told me how they had yet to find who did it

I remembered how your mother passed the same exact way
my goodness how our trauma chases us
how they mentioned this on the news
how no one deserved this
how you didn't deserve this

I came across your picture today
and I remembered us
sitting on my front porch after school,
just the two of us, motherless girls
in plaid skirts
waiting for a brighter tomorrow
I'll remember us this way,
still waiting
for a brighter tomorrow

WHEN THEY SAID SICK

they meant *murder*

as in *your grandmother was sick*

really meant *your grandmother was murdered*

because *you were too young to know*

as in *we couldn't tell you the whole story*

as in *we never found out who did it*

as in *they did an investigation*

as in *case is closed*

as in *cold case*

as in *leave it alone*

wasn't meant for you to know

don't go snooping about business

that is not your business

she's been gone now for so long

we buried her

like we buried the memory

stories with too many legs

be careful what you chase

it may chase you back

I KEEP TRYING TO WRITE ABOUT THE TRAUMA, BUT THE JOY WON'T LET ME

I keep trying to write about the trauma, *but the joy won't let me*
I keep trying to write about the trauma, *but the joy won't let me*
I keep trying to write about the trauma, *but the joy won't let me*
    trying to write about the trauma, *but the joy won't let me*
    trying to write about the trauma, *but the joy won't let me*
    trying to write about the trauma, *but the joy won't let me*
        write about the trauma, *but the joy won't let me*
        write about the trauma, *but the joy won't let me*
            the trauma, *but the joy won't let me*
            the trauma, *but the joy won't let me*
                but the joy won't let me
                but the joy won't let me
                    joy won't let me
                    joy won't let me

RUNNING

i just kept chasing life
when death tried to chase me

i kept trying to write out all the trauma,
but the joy wouldn't let me,

joy in my teeth
spread out like the sun rays
running towards brighter days
even when life is a cathedral of confusion,

you can't outrun destiny
you can't outrun your purpose
joy is in the belly of a riot

how He took life with one hand,
and birthed with another
buried my brother, yet watched
the birth of my niece

peace, must be my portion
freedom my every song
breathe light into dark spaces

even when the cages be our own chests
barbed wire around our hearts

> *joy in the belly of a riot*
> *a riot in the midst of the storm*

i promise life is your birthright
healing is your portion
Love, chases after you

my grandmother's voice is a piano in my throat
my father's laughter is a guitar chord i am learning to play
my aunt called to tell me she loved me today
and my niece asks me when i am coming home

> *joy is in the belly of a riot*
> *joy is a riot in the midst of the storm*
> *and we are finding our way back home*

Eden, our birthright
we are every garden we were birthed into
every word, a new fruit falling from our tongues
and we get to begin again,
find hope again
be joy again
dream a brighter dream
and then dream again

joy is your birthright
healing is your portion
Love, chases after you

joy is your birthright
peace is your portion
Love, chases after you

III. WHEN IT ALL WENT TO FIRE

riot

a violent public disorder

a disturbance of public peace

tumult

ROSES FOR BEA

We knew there were always the snakes. Hiding in bushes and backroad cornfields. How they lifted up their heads and chased people. As if they had a mind of their own. They probably had minds of their own. Then there were the cats. How her brothers tied their tails together or to a fence and watched them fight. Something to entertain the whole neighborhood of kids living inside one house. There was always the house. The outhouse. The shed. The farm. The corn. The cotton. The blood. Oh the blood. *Whose name did it sign again?* The gospel. The spirit. The ghost(s). Some holy. Some still searching the earth to fill their holes. *What was left behind? What do we all leave behind?* When we go… wherever we go. She always told me of the blood. The way the needles in the cotton pricked her fingers, thumb. The pain. That stops you in your tracks. That throws you off your routine. That makes you forget what you were doing or why you were doing it. That makes you wish you weren't. Or maybe never were. The pinch. Piercing through flesh, like a needle in a rose. Or a bush full of snakes. That you can't fully see.

ANGELS FOR RAY

legend has it
that he was dangling over the bridge,
at least half his body
preparing to submerge whole
surrender to whatever darkness could lift the one he was under,
my grandfather walked the normal way home from the bar
but that night, the alcohol became his hands, legs, footsteps
she said she saw him walking
a rag doll flinging himself over a bridge
a kite bending itself into a purple midnight
they said it was after midnight
she arrived, a curly-haired petite woman
carrying him in her arms like a child
a rag doll dangling,
her arms, a bridge
as she told my grandmother how she found him, where… she found him
that she couldn't leave him there alone
we were told they laid him on the couch,
got him settled
when they went back to the door to thank the curly-haired woman
there was no curly-haired woman to be found
no trace, no car
no person

no body, except my grandfather's, safe
nestled back into his home,
back into his skin,
back into his right mind
another chance at life
how he remembered she smelled of lavender,
legend has it, that she must have had wings
that they must have been entertaining
something from
the Heavens

NEVER CALL THE POLICE

She says, "I don't want to just do the abolition work,
I want to do the work of healing"
But what if the abolition work *is* the work of healing?
I don't want to just be the protest
I want to be the prayer
But what if the protest is the prayer?
What if the prayer *is* the protest on fire at the base of everyone's throat?
When our voices are on fire
We become a prayer, an upper room cathedral of torch and chains breaking
When I pray, I am a chain breaking
Breaking the noose off of everyone's wrists
Can you raise them high?
Shout Amen when the hallelujah falls in your palms?
Out of your mouth is a native song
A reminder of everything you've been forced to be outside of your body
And maybe abolition is just that, a calling back into your own body
And maybe we are just that,
Us calling ourselves back into our own bodies
When I wake up, will I raise my flag
Will I remorse for the blood on my hands?
The smoke signals I failed to sound off
The dog whistles that came from my own throat?
When he threatened to come to my house with a gun,

I did not call the police
I did not call the police
I did not call the police
I called his mentors, the elders, my brothers to intervene
I did not call the police
When he threatened to kick us all out, to leave the house,
locked himself in his room with the pistol
We did not call the police
We dare not call the police
Why call the police?
When the men came on my porch, crowbar in hand,
I called my auntie
I called my uncle
I reached for the emergency button
I did not call the police, until she told me to call the police
And then the police came at the same time she did
Which tells me that we can get to Justice at the same time, if we call for Justice

With the same mind
Same sound
Our voices a riot catching fire

HANDS UP: SOMEONE'S PRAISE

when the hands go up
in the flash of a siren
or a *"don't shoot"*
it could be a *"hallelujah"*

it could be   a praise

an unearthing shriek   in the air
a pierce   into the clouds
a line of blood   cutting across the sky
a voice   carving out a home for itself
in the middle   of the air
limbs suspended   in the air
finding right from left   split from each other
both fighting   to climb inside a light
that was not built   for them
a darkness clothed in   a skin bearing their name
a heaviness   perched on a church pew
when the gospel   goes up   sometimes
the bullets   still fall down
the blessings   only a sound   dreams
sweating from skin   running in the middle of the night

trying to find a home in the only home we know
we are trying to find home *in the only home we know*

it could be a siren it could be a *"don't shoot"*
it could be a worship leader's command
a prayered posture a posture that is the prayer
a plead for life a life all pleaded out
it could be *a life all bleeded out*

in the flash of lights they could be *hallelujahs*
they could be "don't shoot"
they could be a surrender, a praise
either depth they someone prays

HOW MUCH HE WANTED SO DEEPLY FOR ME TO BE AN OBEDIENT WIFE

it is always the body that remembers first,
the brain reminds me last
when I forget the exact date,
my body will remind me of my past
I said "forever"
he said "for   ever?"
a covenant turned crossroad
a conviction turned crucifixion
all the promises are running backwards
down my throat
I am pulling red flags from my mouth
when he told me I was worthless,
I made the excuse
when he left me at the restaurant to
teach me the lesson,
I said he didn't mean it
when he told me I had to leave the house,
stole the money from the bank
brought the shotgun to my bedside,
I stopped going to sleep
after the surgery, he sent flowers
told the doctors how sorry he was

how much he loved me
how much he wanted so deeply
for me to be
an obedient wife
when we said "forever"
we were already broken in half
shattered words spread out on a glass altar
a memory collapsing in our regrets
a splintered "ever"
that was never
"for" us

I THINK OF THE GIRL IN THE GREEN DRESS

the lace trim around the edge
bright eyes and ribbons in her hair
before she learned to grow into the shape
of your face
this is how I remember your humanity
that you too were once a young girl
learning to brave the earth with no direction
a mother who knew not how to be a mother
a father who held the alcohol bottle as if
it was his wife
I remember that you didn't get many years
to just be the girl
to just be the child with youth in her eyes
a dream perched in her teeth

Two:
you never told me about the first time he hit you
you only told me about the time you got away
and never went back
the long-sleeved turtlenecks to hide the bruises
on arms and neck
you told me how you got pregnant the very first time
that it only takes one time

and the second pregnancy was the only reason the
third man proposed
we talked about how there were women, always
women, you never really knew how many
but you let me know
about the night y'all held a rifle to his face
just to make him nervous
or the night you keyed his car once he finally
came home
or the knife you left hanging in his favorite
leather coat, just to remind him
what you were capable of

Three:
people always knew about the fire
we grew up with the wrath
but no one ever questioned where it came from
how many times you were violated
how many babies heaven stole back from your womb
how many funerals you actually had to plan
how many tears you had to surrender back to God

Four:
when we think of you now
we often hear of your loneliness
the way you take out your pain
we hear the blame, the fear

of dying alone
of being left with no one to care for you
how you sacrificed many dreams, so that we
could be who we are
the way you don't always love who we are
how it takes us away from home
how it stole us from you

Five:
when I don't understand you
when you say things that burn a hole through
my chest
I remember your humanity
that you were once a little girl
wearing a skirt the color of a forest
walking yourself out of a forest
finding your way
back to yourself

HOUSE OF DUST

You will build a house out of dust
until you realize that the home is within you

When I realized I was being swallowed it was too late
I saw the bullet swallow the wind
and I remembered how the clouds
held up the sky
Though I walk through the valley of the shadow of death,
I am reminded that it is just that,
A shadow
That these dry bones can still rise on tomorrow

Told Death,
you thought you had all of me,
How I buried my mother at 15, watched my brother take his last breath at 17,
visited my father on psych floors of hospital rooms for years,
Then I ran into houses of men disguised like homes,

You will build a house out of dust until you realize the home is within you,

When you pain out loud,
And there's pain in your body the size of a whale,

stuck inside the whale, my body drifts and floats around me,
Tell Jonah, how I swallowed myself into the belly of my own fear,
and woke up swimming in the reality of my insecurity's scales,
Now all I see is shadow of myself,

I lived, broken girl, and made all the wrong choices
How I moved out of my house, into her house, to his house,
into hotels, and couches,
from home to home, to house to house, to where is my home?
Is there a home etched inside a staccato for me?

Oh Lord, I want to forgive the man who raised his hand,
forgive the broken black boy who had his back broken, so he broke mine,
Failed to see I was rib, so he broke my spine,
Forgive the black boy broken whose daddy loved him hollow,
so he hunts for housewives made of sheepskin
and tongueless mouths,
Father, forgive him, for he knows not what he does,
Father forgive me, for I knew not who I was,

I flooded my bones with suicide,
and every demon who whispered into my eardrum
Staccatoed opinions that almost swallowed me whole,
How I learned to build a house out of dust
until I realized the home was within me

Then one day,
I stopped doing all the things I thought I had to do,
Stopped being all the things I thought I needed to be,
Remembered, how I could write myself out of my own skin,
My mouth, a boundary worth breaking
Remembered what it was like,
To have poems written into me,
To write myself into a poem so thick it spills salvation
To cough so many poems from my lungs that it creates sanctuary,
Yea, though I walk through the valley of the shadow of death,
I will no longer fear myself,

What a sacrifice,
to go to every dark place
and have to write life
back into your life
just for someone else to breathe

Oh Jonah, I know you ran
from what would carve you holy,
For you didn't understand that
the calling will always outrun you
My chaos was birthed
in every ounce of normalcy
I thought I needed to be

When my freedom was just found
in just being me

Here, is where I throw up my hands, and tell myself to dance,
Until every piece of devil that was burned within me falls into landing

When the neighbors told me of my house,
I said my house of dust blew up in flames
while I was inside,
but I survived,
Told them of the shadows,
showed them my scales,
That I was searching for house through all of this dust,
Until I learned to find the home within myself

MAY DIES IN APRIL

She was my auntie's favorite auntie. Everyone wanted to be like her. How she smelled of hibiscus and magnolia. Summertime and a lemonade smile. At least that's what I gather from the pictures. My auntie is a sweet sassy one. Born in May. Her favorite Auntie, named May, was born in a broken tooth winter. The kind of skin even the seasons escape. She lived a life. And loved hard. Yet, was the sweetest sort of spring. Her mouth. Always in bloom. And right when the seasons changed. When the snow began to ease off the Midwest ground. When the sky became a little clearer and it all turned to rain, with the sun peeking her eyes out during the day. And all the flowers began opening their mouths towards the sky. She opened her mouth up to heaven. Her face wide towards all the blue. So wide, you could fit a cloud in it. So wide you could see all the prayers crawling upward. Like a ladder. Her body. Stiff and still, like a ladder. The birds were chirping again. It was finally Spring. And May was gone. May died in the Spring.

I AM NOT MY GRIEF

i am not my grief

grief is often a body i cannot crawl out of

i am not this body
i am not this body

grief is not my portion
grief does not own me
grief is not my name
grief is not a house

i am not this house of grief surrounding me
i am but a door
i am but a window
i am but a glimmer of light
climbing through a breeze

a Sunday morning full of tomorrows
in the depths of grief, i will remember
that there is still a tomorrow

i am not this grief that tries to own me
i am not this grief that tries to hold me
in the depths of all this grief

i can still be a small fist
a small breath of hope climbing into the sky
climbing towards another morning
joy, creeping out
from the soil

HOW DO I TELL YOU EVERYTHING AND KEEP MYSELF FROM SPILLING?

when the emotion is too much
we become the bridge's back
the anchor to bite down and hold
the entire list of words curling from
a mouth, the cradle
that crawls into itself, the wombs
that break open before their time

they say timing is everything
how do we fully begin when we are
ending the story already? our words
can't seem to find each other on the
right roads, our lanes intersect
and miss each other at midnight
how do I fully trust (you) again?

how do I open myself up like a prayer
that always seems to go unanswered?
how do I tell you everything and keep
myself from spilling out onto everything?
how do I tell you how afraid I am?

that fear is a wind that chases me,
a cloud I cannot seem to escape

I want to be a good friend, but I
am constantly being challenged by
who I am not. I know I should have been
excited about what you wanted to say
but fear became a fist in my throat
I am still not able to swallow

WHEN IT ALL WENT TO FIRE

I wrote myself into a prayer

I escaped into a new kind of word
a new kind of language

one with a pathway to heaven
a journey towards something larger than myself

when all I knew was death,
I had to do everything in my power

to find even a small dose of life
with a new version of life

on my tongue, I found myself crouched
down into a small bedroom corner

rocking myself to sleep, my pen
moving back and forth while I was shaking

writing my way into a new kind of freedom
when it all went to fire,

I tucked my body into an Amen.
everything around me in flames

yet finding peace in the middle of my small
corner of hope, I found a poem

in the middle of talking to God,
I found prayer in the sacredness of a poem

I found God, in the purest form of
trying to find myself

in the pursuit of anything that hadn't
already blown into smoke.

IV. THERE MUST BE ANGELS WALKING WITH ME

joy

happiness over an unanticipated or present good

a source or cause of delight

state of contentment and peace

I AM NOT WHAT MY FAMILY HAS DONE

I am not what my family has done
I am not what my family has been through
I am not what I have been through
I am not what I have survived
I am not my trauma
I am not *only* the stories singing from my bloodline

IF NOT THIS RIVER AND OCEAN

if not this ocean
a flood, pouring and
runneth over

our mouths too much
tornado for the scenery
surrounding us, the skin
carved mirage on top of
everything we know to be

once she is in the ground
whose daughter do you become?
are you still someone's daughter?
are you anything more
than gaping wound left open?

has your gaping wound ever become
an ocean?
a flood that runneth, pouring
over into someone's mouth?
has your wound ever become a mouth?

tornadoing through everything that
surrounds you
everyone that tries to become skin
spread over grief?
love can sometimes appear mirage
when the wound

is the only thing
we know to be

WHAT IS A BODY EXCEPT TO BE

except to be sacrificed for another body

except to be given up for a friend

except to be laid down and stretched out

except to be broken into bones, dust

except to be shattered into silence, sand

except to be an ocean pouring from the mouth

except to be peace dancing in the middle of a storm

except to be the harshest death of night bursting into

a sky full of lights surrounding us

twirling us into a new tomorrow

except to be a new encounter

except to be a new acceptance

accept to be into the sound of something more

accept these bones into new doors, thrusted

accept into silence shattered into skies, open

accept into a peace, walking in the midst of every storm

accept the darkest night of a death, until only light spits back

until the body is so full of sacrifice

only light shouts back

WHEN SHE SAYS "MY BODY"

she means "mine" as in "has always been"
as in "operates from my own function, own strength"
own hands
there is no price tag for this
no noose to wrap around neck
here, we get to own what comes inside and what leaves
what breathes and what bleeds

when she says, "my body" she means
decisions get to be made
and judgements must swallow themselves
she means she will not swallow herself
on an ocean floor, a sea of voices floating around her

when she says "body," she means "temple"
"vessel" the right to live out a life's purpose

how do we use faith as a weapon to pass judgement?
how can you shout Black Lives Matter around the blood pouring in the streets
and dismiss the teenage girl being tortured by a man in her sleep?
the woman's body being bruised by her husband's fist
until she has more children

the woman who just wants to say "not now"
the woman who says "today" and the ability to raise her child
in her own beautiful way
where support is not a suggestion
where violence is no longer an option
for Black and Brown bodies
where you can have faith and fruition
where you can still praise your God and still respect everyone's decisions,

When I say, "my body" what I really mean is
Today, I get to choose me,
Today, freedom is an outstretched palm
a prayer the day after
someone who held my hand in the clinic
the counselor who had the courage to tell me "the next time, he will hit you"
the open door
the right to walk through it
the right to say "not now"
the option to say "I don't want to"
the voice to say "I choose me"
and really be heard

When we say "our bodies"
We mean choose
We mean freedom
We mean "who gets to own yours?"

We mean nobody owns our bodies but us
We mean God's image
We shout God's image
Until we truly see it in ourselves
And remember we are more than what they have told us
More than how they have treated us
More than what we somedays claim ourselves
Name ourselves

we're saying, no one gets to remove us from this land
no one gets to uproot us from a land
even if the land is within our own skin

to say, "my body" is
to feel safe within my own skin
to make the decisions I need to make
that are best for my life
and any life that calls itself forth from me
it is to say, "my life matters"
"your life matters"
"you matter"

your body is a cathedral
nothing but light pours through
which is to say, you are a torch
here to guide others along the journey

it is to say,
someone's life depends on your light
someone's light is waiting on your fight
someone's life is depending on your fight

I CHOOSE TO HEAL BECAUSE I CAN

the morning greeted me with a new opportunity

to shed the skin of yesterday

of everything I was

of everyone I was not able to be

and I praise God for who I am today

for the opportunity that exists within each breath

today, I choose to heal

to walk into the journey of the unknown

to walk into who I know I can be

to visualize a healed version of myself

to believe that a healed version of myself actually exists

to witness her dancing, breathing, living, being free

to know that it is possible

to release everything that is no longer serving

the version of the brokenness that so often wants to yield fruit

to continue planting seeds of life

that every part of who I know I can be

every ounce of who I know I want to be

can bloom

I choose to heal

I choose me

TOO MUCH/NO ONE CAN TELL ME NOTHING: AN ODE AND ELEGY FOR THE PERM

I am not certain of the age, but I am certain that it was afterschool
perhaps a kindergarten kind of day
the brown and yellow plaid skirt in the picture tells me that I was
flexing in this all day, smelling like outside
with all of outside dancing its way through my hair

my hair, too tight
my hair, too kinky
my hair, too much to comb
take too long to straighten
too much heat to make it comb-able
too many tears, I must have cried
mama and grandma tried

but grandma did not play
"you can smell like outside, but you best be lookin like something
when you takin your behind outside"
so here we are, at Press & Kurl hair salon on the southside
of Y-town, every two weeks to make sure
we had ourselves christened right, under the right light,
right heat, right smell of everything familiar

and clean and proper in the world
and it was my Friday to be initiated

and grandma was proper, okay?
never left the house without a pristine red lip
and hair parted to the side, slicked down
pantyhose and heels,
and if she wore pants, there were creases, always
creases starched to perfection,
a jewel hanging from each earlobe
and white diamonds perched around her neck
like the perfume was made for her
I'm sure she sweated white diamonds

but back to my kindergarten Friday, this day
was for me and my hair
it was my turn to sit still
my legs dangling from the seat, perched
all the way up high, I could see on top of everyone's head
above all the dryers
above every shower cap and white paper taped
around edges and wrap-lotion
around everyone falling asleep
drifting to the sound of the loud hum around
their ears, or those reading Jet Magazine or Ebony or The Source
or Vibe

for me, this was my vibe
I remember how it felt, cold on edges
a comb slicing parts across my scalp
Ms. Paulette and her gloves
the gray and black plastic wrapped around me
to cover my clothes
almost like I am at the dentist
but I am not at the dentist

although I am discovering new ways to smile
at myself in the mirror
a new life is being created for me
"let me know if it burns," she says
and I am okay for a while, until I am not
and it is time to wash all the white from my hair
and miraculously, miraculously?
my hair is no longer difficult
my hair is no longer strange
no longer too kinky
no longer too hard to tame
no longer too much

I am no longer too much
I am a dryer set and a curling iron away from
being *"just right"* or *"presentable"*
I am Shirley Temple curls or waves
I am a wrap with a part to the side

I am pin curls, some up, some down
a French roll if I want to keep
my hairstyle for longer than a week
or my favorite, flat twists all around
and untwist them once you come out
from under the dryer
and your hair is just wavy
doesn't everyone want their hair just wavy?

I am in kindergarten and
I have finally been initiated
I am now an every-two-weeks girl
I can now pick out styles

my hair is no longer difficult
I am no longer difficult

I am now one of the pretty ones
one of the kept ones
one of the ones the white girls compliment
even though I still can't get my hair wet

I am presentable
I am inside
I smell like inside
I am no longer too much time
I am just enough time

I am no longer pull and stretch and tame, tame, tame
I am tamed
I might as well have a new name
I am a new flame caught in a little boy's eye
I am no woman, no cry
I am a flutter in my own new sky
I have a new sky
I have a new world
I am a new world

and no one
can tell me
nothing

YOU ARE A PRAYER

you are a prayer
your mouth is garden
belly of seeds unravel
like survival
today, you live
a new sky
bodies unfold like
petals under the
sun's stems
you are worth
every today's breath
every wind
that consumes
your lungs,
you deserve
every seed
of healing
yours to water
you are worth
every ounce
every right
to bloom

THERE MUST BE ANGELS WALKING WITH ME

                                                  I used to   wake up

fighting demons   in my sleep

    funerals, a parade
in my dreams

      emergency button above my bed
              a crescendo
                      of bullets
                          cas-
                              -cading the sky
but we were kept alive

            can't you see, there are angels walking with me?

devil tried to
swallow

me whole
        claim   my   life

but God told death, *"she's mine"*

      sound of burning buildings

          all the dreams about caskets,

                  and then I had to pick out my mother's

     but when he had the gun

     to my head,

          the bullet

              never
                  released

     when the men on porch

         crowbar in hand,
         they weren't able

            to shatter the glass

                this body

     stray bullets

         never caught any of us

        by the throat

all limbs   still left   in tact

        every weapon that formed,

        but did not prosper

can't you see, how there are angels walking with me?

    parting the sea   of every storm

like a mouth

    with a praise

        pouring out

there are warriors in my blood

   a cloud of giants chanting in ancestor rhythms

surrounding my sleep and my day

   my back and before

there are generations

speaking through me

a swarm of swords swinging

from my mouth

a lineage of prayers

falling from my tongue

know that there are angels carrying me

can't you see, how there are angels walking with me?

V. HERE IS WHERE I THROW UP MY HANDS AND TELL MYSELF TO DANCE

and *joy* still

"joy is not the absence of pain, but it's happiness in spite of it"

GIVE ME A HOME

give me a settling
give me my mother's life
which has always been good enough for me
her life without the drama
without the pain
without the cancer
give me a real home
a house to come home to
home that I can say is my home
someone waiting for me
a few children and dinner to make
a dinner to be made, grocery store nearby
to make it,
give me a porch, a swing in summertime
a summertime even in the midst of winter
I can feel the sun, the light
the warmth of everything that calls me back
wants me back
needs me to come back
to make it home safe
at the core of who I am, I have always wanted the safe, the love
a dream swollen in my chest, God who dreams bigger dreams for me
than I could dream for myself

make a wife out of me,
make a mother out of me
let this peace break into me so softly
it creates new life
let new life find home inside me
find the warmth in my soft
find the soft in places where I no longer
have to be hard
have to protect
can't be gentle
let me be gentle
be subtle
be supple
be front door and window
screen door flinging open
when it's hot outside
be the rain, especially when
it's hot outside
give me the inside of you
every emotion, every fear
every tear tucked soft, tucked
hard, tucked under the grief,
the abandonment, the rage,
and the joy
let's find the joy and learn
to swim in it
choose to walk on it even

when we're watching the boats sink
around us, even when
the waves crash against us
let us lean against each other
let us grow into each other
let us be a foundation
a fortress
a home
a home
to come home to

you asked about the porch
and today, I want it

HERE IS THE SURRENDER IN FORGIVENESS

the release of letting go
of breathing out everything I cannot control
and breathing in the only things in my power
the choice to react
the opportunity to respond
the ability to release
here is where I choose to let go
to release everything that I could not control
to release every broken heart that broke mine
to let go of every broken vessel that shattered me
in attempt to survive their own journey
here is where I allow my own journey
to be exactly what it needs to be
to release the secrets of my family's past
to let go of all the things that harmed my bloodline
to shake off everything I do not know
here is where I choose to surrender
here is where I choose to forgive
here is where I bless the blood that flows
bless the blood that loves me back
bless the blood that borrows my bones
for comfort, for covering, for life
here is the surrender in releasing

everything that no longer serves you
of taking back everything you are
and everything you can become
here is the surrender of every
version of you that you are not
to surrender into everything you are

A NEW APPETITE

I only remember the snow
the long drive back
the cold and dark roads that led us
there… everywhere
we decided on a hotel
the closest we could find
how it was too icy to drive home

I was never afraid to stay with you
close, just the two of us
my aunt was thankful that at least I
wasn't by myself, at least you were with me

it was an Amish hotel, I think
a country dark road, out in the middle of nowhere
we were in the middle of nowhere
a back road trailing the backside of an Ohio city

there was a bookstand as we entered,
near the receptionist
and I picked up the book, the first book I
have ever read on fasting, I had

never understood fasting
until that day

I remember the smells
the smells trapped in your jeans as you flopped them
on the bed, the food smells
wading out of your suitcase
they were different from mine
everything was now different from mine

me and that book,
a new language twirling around my tongue
a new way to grow closer to a God
my soul wanted to know, even when my flesh
did not understand

that book changed my life
in just a few pages, in just a few words
how a book on fasting
could give me a whole new appetite
I remember, God
was always with me

MAY WE NEVER FORGET TO HOLD FAST TO WHO WE ARE

to who we know we are called to be
to the tiny voice within that reminds us of our reflection
calls us back into our own skin
when the ocean is breaking inside of us
remember the spine is often a bridge
that there have been seeds planted for generations
that we can water our own soil

your mouth is a garden
spitting out stems like prayers
every prayer falling off your tongue
is a new life you get to walk into
may you never forget who you are
that there is true power inside of you
that you were built for more than what the earth
has offered you

that grief is not a cloak you have to wear
death is not the shade of your skin
burden is not the shape of your bones
you are more than what has unearthed before you
that your feet be shod with sanity

that your sanity is a miracle
your every new step, a new ground made holy

may you never forget you are holy
made in an image that chases after you
like love
finding her way back into everyone's throat
slipping through the backdoors of backbones
and heart chambers

just to remind us who we are
may you remember who you are
that you are a calling being fulfilled
a journey harvesting in every season
a new rain
ready to bloom

I CHOOSE TO LIVE

> I choose to live
> Today, I choose to live
> Today, I choose to live
> Today, I choose life
> Today, I choose life

BLESS THE CHILD

you never got to the chance to be
mourn her,
take her hand and run with her
into a place of safety
the only safety you have ever known

bless the child who has never known safety
bless the little child who lives inside you
the one who never had the chance
to cry from a place of freedom

bless the child who has never known freedom
wings sprouted from the shoulder blades
of the bodies that caught bullets too soon
bless the bodies of children who caught bullets too soon

bless the younger you who was caught in the fire
the abandonment, the pain, the grief, the abuse
release your younger self from the fire
release the abandonment, the pain, the grief, the abuse
release every ounce of what no longer serves you

bless the bones that are growing beyond the trauma
bless the child that sprouts joy from her feet
bless the child who was always a seed
watered by the world, set ablaze by the sun

bless the one who was you
bless the child that was you
bless the child that lives inside you
bless the body that has harnessed you
bless the you that has survived
bless the child that kept you
long enough for you to get here
bless the you that is here
bless the you that is here
bless the you

THERE IS A WAY TO BE WHOLE AGAIN

a belly is often a field of grief
a valley that sits in the middle of the seams
a journey that is never easy, whispering
there is a way to be whole again

to be whole again is to say:
I release myself from the fear
I release myself from the grief
I release myself from the pain

even in the release of the trauma,
there can still be a peace
love can still live here
my limbs can still find a rhythm here

dance in the middle of the street
of my own sacred surrender
the surrender will always sing back to me
there is a way to be whole again

when my skin sings back to me
a song I may not want to hear

I find a rhythm that holds my heart
tell my heart to remind my brain,

there is a way to be whole again
there is always a way to be whole
healing is a life's journey
wholeness is a birthright

when the wholeness seems too far away
I release myself into the freedoms
that call me back into myself
I turn myself into the prayer,

shouting, singing, dancing,
whispering, rhythming, calling,
silencing, thrusting, howling,
there is a way to be whole again

BE THE JOY

*for every vessel that has desired to move
towards their healing journey,
this is for you,
a prayer etched into the body of a poem,
this is for you*

*you are the spark crackling amongst the darkness
the glimmer lighting someone's path home
when the silence is a body of skin stretched around you like a siren
in the middle of the riot, you are the joy
in the center of the riot, you will be the joy
in the belly of the riot, be the joy*

ACKNOWLEDGMENTS

To God be the Glory for this book! I am thankful that the Lord chose me as a vessel and gave me poetry, so that I could write my way into freedom and through my own healing process.

Thank you so much to all those who have published my work in the past, including Penmanship Books, Sundress Publications, Academy of American Poets, *Electric Literature*, *Harness Magazine*, *The McNeese Review*, The Ohio State University Press, and Button Poetry.

I am incredibly humbled and grateful to Moore Black Press, Serendipity Lit, Amistad, and the entire HarperCollins team for believing in this work and for believing in me. To jessica Care moore, Brad Walrond, Regina Brooks, Emma Loy-Santelli, Abby West, Makayla Tabron, thank you, thank you, thank you. Thank you for your faith in this work and in me, for advocating, and for making sure this book is in the world.

I am thankful to all the organizations that have supported me and lifted me up during these last several years, including Afro Unidad, ArtHype, Arts for Healing and Justice Network, Beyond Baroque, Black Women for Wellness, Coleman Health Services, The Columbus Foundation, Favour Consulting, Flourish Agenda, Greater Columbus Arts Council, the Giovanni Collective, Harmony Project Columbus, Homeboy Art Academy, Just Media, LionLike Mindstate, Maroon Arts Group, Methodist Theological School, Matter News, NOAH, Ohio Arts Council, Project Knucklehead, Rhythm Arts

Alliance, Streetlight Guild, Street Poets Inc., Thiossane West African Dance Institute, Thurber House, Transit Arts, Youngstown Public Library, and Zora's House.

Immense gratitude to the community who has shaped my life, those that have poured into me, those that have spoken life over me. To Mahogany L. Browne, Sunni Patterson, Khadijah Queen, Hanif Abdurraqib, Airea D. Matthews, Will Evans, Scott Woods, Kaleem Musa, Maggie Smith, Jive Poetic, Ajanae Dawkins, Tiffani Smith, Caroline Rothstein, Rico Frederick: thank you for loving me and for calling me back into myself.

To ONE LA and Believe LA, thank you for being family and for reminding me of the power of faith communities. To my Ohio and my California family, thank you for holding me up, always.

To the blood-born & blood-chosen, thank you for always holding up the mirror, for reminding me of who I am, and calling me into who I am becoming.

To Is Said, there is no me without you. To MarShawn McCarrel and Amber Evans, I am a better vessel because of your fire.

To my grandmothers, Lonnie Belle and Beatrice, and my mother Jacqueline, none of this would be possible without you. Thank you for walking in boldness and for giving birth again and again.

To those who read this work, may you continue to walk forward in your journey, may you learn to embrace and love your journey, to say yes to God and yes to you, may you thrive, Beloved. And even in the belly of the riot, even when the riot may be inside you, may you remain, may you persevere, may you be the joy.